Anonymus

Alabama Institute for the Deaf and the Blind

Anonymus

Alabama Institute for the Deaf and the Blind

ISBN/EAN: 9783741177767

Manufactured in Europe, USA, Canada, Australia, Japa

Cover: Foto ©Thomas Meinert / pixelio.de

Manufactured and distributed by brebook publishing software
(www.brebook.com)

Anonymus

Alabama Institute for the Deaf and the Blind

BIENNIAL ❀ REPORT

(THIRTY-FIFTH AND THIRTY-SIXTH ANNUAL REPORTS)

——OF THE——

BOARD ⊹ OF ⊹ TRUSTEES

——OF THE——

Alabama Institute for the Deaf,

IN CHARGE OF THE

Alabama Institute for the Deaf,

Alabama Academy for the Blind.

——AND THE——

Ala. School for Negro Deaf-Mutes & Blind,

TO THE GOVERNOR.

1896.

— ∙∙∙❖∙∙∙

PRINTED BY THE PUPILS AT THE ALABAMA INSTITUTE FOR THE DEAF
TALLADEGA. ALA.

BOARD OF TRUSTEES.

ALABAMA INSTITUTE FOR THE DEAF.

OFFICERS AND TEACHERS.

PRINCIPAL:

J. H. Johnson.

TEACHERS:

MANUAL DEPARTMENT:

S. J. Johnson,　　Osce Roberts,　　Miss A. L. Johnson,
W. S. Johnson,　　　　Miss M. E. Toney.

ORAL DEPARTMENT:

Miss Vivian May.　　　　　　J. F. Bledsoe.
　　Miss O. E. D. Hart,　　T. S. McAloney.

INDUSTRIAL DEPARTMENT:

Osce Roberts,　-　-　-　Foreman Printing Office.
M. J. Hingle,　-　-　-　-　Master Mechanic.
W. G. Davirson,　-　-　-　Machinist.
John Lennard.　-　-　-　-　Gardener
Miss Emma Ruppert.　-　-　Seamstress.
Smith Williams, -　-　-　-　Cook.

DOMESTIC DEPARTMENT:

J. H. Johnson.　-　-　-　-　-　Superintendent.
Mrs. S. M. Montgomery.　-　-　-　Matron.
Miss Mary Rhyne.　-　-　-　-　Housekeeper.
Miss Mary Toney.　-　-　-　-　-　Girls' Supervisor
John Lennard.　-　-　-　-　-　Boys' Supervisor.
Hill Benagh.　-　-　-　-　-　Boys' Supervisor.
W. G. Davirson.　-　-　-　-　-　Engineer.

ALABAMA ACADEMY FOR THE BLIND.

OFFICERS AND TEACHERS.

PRINCIPAL:

J. H. Johnson.

ASSISTANT PRINCIPAL

F. H. Manning.

TEACHERS

INTELLECTUAL DEPARTMENT

F. H. Manning,   Miss Lilah McDaniel,
Miss Annie Brockman,   Miss Fanny Leonard.

MUSICAL DEPARTMENT

J. S. Laverty,   A. W. Williams,
                       Thos. L. Williams.

INDUSTRIAL DEPARTMENT

Chas. Petty,   -   -   -   -   -   - Master Shops.
Miss Bonner, -   -   -   -   -   -   - Seamstress.

DOMESTIC DEPARTMENT

F. H. Manning,   -   -   Resident Superintendent.
Mrs. F. H. Manning, -   - Matron.
Mrs. V. A. Hamill,   -   Housekeeper.
Miss Bonner,   -   -   - Girls' Supervisor.
Q. D. Brown, -   -   - Engineer and Boys' Supervisor.

ALABAMA SCHOOL FOR THE NEGRO DEAF-MUTES AND BLIND.

OFFICERS AND TEACHERS.

PRINCIPAL

J. H. Johnson

ASSISTANT PRINCIPAL

J. S. Graves.

TEACHERS:

INTELLECTUAL DEPARTMENT:

J. S. Graves. - - - - Teacher of the Blind.
George Thomason - - - - Teacher of the Blind.
A. F. Wood. - - - - - Teacher of the Deaf.

MUSICAL DEPARTMENT:

George Thomason. - - - - - - Teacher.

INDUSTRIAL DEPARTMENT:

J. W. Rogers. - - - - - - Master Shops.

DOMESTIC DEPARTMENT:

J. S. Graves. - - - - Resident Superintendent.
Mrs. Olla Graves. - - - Matron.
A. F. Wood. - - - - Supervisor.
Mrs. Patterson. - - - - Housekeeper.

PRESIDENT'S REPORT

TALLADEGA, ALA., October 1st, 1896.

To HON. WM. C. OATES,

Governor of Alabama:

Herewith I have the honor to submit to you the Thirty-Fifth and Thirty-Sixth Annual Reports of the Principal and Officers of the Alabama Institute for the Deaf and Blind.

It is with grateful satisfaction that I am able to call your attention to the prosperous condition of the three Institutions.

Never before in their history, has the number of pupils in attendance been so great, or their advancement more satisfactory.

So material has been the accession of pupils, that the resources of the officers have been taxed to find room for all without overcrowding in the sleeping apartments. To relieve this condition, the Board of Trustees are making constant efforts, with the limited means at their command, to increase the dormitory capacity

The sanitary condition of the school is all that can be reasonably expected, with the exception of a mild form of epidemic measles last spring, the general health has been excellent.

The official announcement of the death of Hon. S. K. McSpadden, a fellow trustee, which occurred May 3rd, 1896, is made with profound sadness. Appropriate resolutions, with a brief biographical sketch of our departed co-laborer were prepared and adopted by the Board of Trustees, and will be found accompanying this communication.

The past high efficiency in the administration of these State schools, it is gratifying to state is fully maintained;

attesting in an eminent degree the capable efficiency of the present management.

In the Treasurer's report will be found a detailed account, and correct statement of all moneys received and disbursed by that officer.

The enrollment of pupils, with suggestions, and report upon the general management of the school, will be found in the Report of the Principal and his faithful subordinates.

Invoking the continued generous support of the General Assembly in behalf of these Institutions, and the continuance of your high consideration, I have the honor to be,

Very respectfully your obedient servant,

W. TAYLOR,
President Board of Trustees

REPORT OF THE SECRETARY OF THE
BOARD OF TRUSTEES.

TALLADEGA, ALA., OCTOBER 1st. 1896

DR. WM. TAYLOR,
President Board of Trustees of the
Alabama Institute for the Deaf:

I have the honor herewith to submit to you the Report of the Treasurer of the Board as required by law for the two fiscal years just past, ending September 30th, 1896. And also by order of the Board of Trustees the Report of the Principal, as to the management and progress of the three schools under his supervision, for the same period of time.

Respectfully submitted,

J. H. JOHNSON,
Secretary of the Board of Trustees

GROUNDS, ALABAMA INSTITUTE FOR THE DEAF.

PRINCIPAL'S REPORT

TALLADEGA, ALA., October 1st, 1896.

To the Board of Trustees

GENTLEMEN:—I have the honor to submit the following report upon the three schools under my care, for the biennial period ending September 30th, 1896.

I report upon the condition and affairs of each school separately, as follows:

ALABAMA INSTITUTE FOR THE DEAF.

ATTENDANCE.

During the two years covered by this report, we have enrolled one hundred and fifty-two pupils—eighty-two boys and seventy girls. Forty-one counties are represented; twenty-five counties are not represented. The pupils in attendance are distributed among the counties represented as follows:

Bullock	2	Limestone	5
Calhoun	7	Lowndes	1
Chambers	6	Madison	7
Cherokee	3	Marshall	3
Choctaw	2	Mobile	2
Clarke	2	Marion	1
Clay	6	Monroe	2
Colbert	4	Montgomery	3
Coffee	2	Morgan	3
Dallas	6	Perry	2
Dale	2	Pike	6
Dekalb	8	Randolph	3
Elmore	4	Russell	2
Etowah	2	Shelby	2
Franklin	2	St Clair	2
Henry	1	Talladega	11
Jackson	3	Tallapoosa	4
Jefferson	16	Tuscaloosa	2
Lauderdale	3	Walker	1
Lamar	2	Wilcox	1
Lawrence	2		

Total 152.

Our attendance is steadily increasing. Our buildings are taxed to their utmost capacity. We very much need more room for dormitories and class-rooms. There are many deaf children in the State who ought to be in our school, and who can be brought in if we had the room for them. It is to be hoped that the Legislature will make the necessary provision for these children as soon as possible.

HEALTH

The general health of our pupils has been good. We have had one death. James Henry Blevins, eight years of age, died of pneumonia, December 2nd, 1891. This is the first death in the school since 1878, and it is the fourth in the history of the Institution. We had sixty cases of measles in the winter of 1895-96; each case made a good recovery. The closest attention is paid to our sanitary arrangements. The grounds are well drained, and are kept scrupulously clean. Great care is taken to keep the pupils comfortable, and to make them cleanly in habits and person. These precautions, together with a healthy locality, wholesome diet, and regular hours, secure for us the enjoyment of health.

STAFF.

In 1894, an additional class becoming necessary, the services of Mr. T. S. McAloney, a fellow of Gallaudet College, were secured.

At the close of the term in June 1895, Miss Mary McGuire, who had been with us for five years, resigned to accept a position in the School for the Deaf at Pittsburg, Pa., at an increased salary. The vacancy thus caused was filled by the appointment of Miss Vivian May.

In January 1896, an increased enrollment made an additional teacher necessary, and we secured the services of Miss Grace D. Ely. In June 1896, Miss Ely resigned to accept a position in the Maryland School over which her father presides. The vacancy, caused by the resignation of Miss Ely, was filled by the appointment of Miss O. E. D. Hart. Miss Hart comes to us from the School for the Deaf at Mt. Airy, Pa.

In November 1895, Miss S. A. Tillinghast resigned her position as matron. The vacancy has been filled by the appoint-

SCHOOL BUILDING, ALABAMA INSTITUTE FOR THE DEAF.

ment of Mrs. S. M. Montgomery, who comes to us having had experience in the Minnesota and Wisconsin Schools.

THE CLASS ROOM.

The number of classes has increased from *seven* to *nine*. We use what is known as the combined system. About sixty per cent. of our pupils are taught speech, and lip-reading.

In five of these classes instruction is carried on by means of speech, using signs and manual spelling when expedient. In four classes signs and manual spelling are relied upon entirely.

Our school is better graded than it has ever been. We are consequently doing better work. It is very probable that we shall get a still better classification during the current year, since the number of applications for admission indicates that additional classes will be necessary. It will be readily understood that the greater number of classes we have, the more chances each pupil will have to find its proper level or grade.

Our classes are well supplied with texts, and apparatus. I have not hesitated to supply the teachers with any aid or appliance that promised to be of benefit to the classes.

We continue, however, to work in class rooms much too small for comfort or convenience. We look forward earnestly to the time when this can be remedied.

INDUSTRIAL DEPARTMENT.

We lay great stress upon this department, and we are glad to report progress in all branches. Some of our carpenter boys show marked improvement, not only in the quality of their work, but also in the rapidity and skill with which it is done.

There are six or eight boys in this department who should be self sustaining in any community.

In the printing office there is a large per cent of small boys who have only recently begun work; several of these promise to make good printers.

We have two of last year's class filling places in the State; one on a weekly, and one on a daily paper. Each of these is self sustaining, and contributes to the support of his family.

The cabinet shops, and and the printing department are well

equipped to do good work. Nothing more is needed in either department except additional floor space.

I am exceedingly anxious to introduce "Sloyd" into our school. I saw the results of "Sloyd" in Philadelphia, Hartford and Boston last fall. I am much impressed with its value.

It is our desire to establish as soon as practicable, a shoe shop. There is no branch of handicraft better suited to the opportunities of the deaf to earn a living after leaving school than shoe making and repairing.

Our boys have the advantage of the girls in the industrial department. The facilities and advantages enjoyed by them are greater than is afforded the girls.

I am glad to say that notwithstanding the fact that their facilities and opportunities are limited, the girls have done remarkably well. They have worked hard, and many of them have become expert with the needle and machine. Many of them can make their own dresses, and some have learned to cut and fit. In addition to plain sewing, all kinds of fancy work, knitting, crocheting, etc., is taught.

We have learned by experience that it is not practicable to have classes in cooking in the same kitchen at the same time that meals are being prepared for the school; at least not until the classes have had some training. We hope in the near future that we can have a room fitted up with stove and other necessary appliances for practical training in culinary work. It is our idea to have our girls taught, not how to make a few fancy dishes, but how to prepare and cook properly any common dish or article of food.

GIRLS' EXHIBIT, TERM 1894-95.

Aprons, Boys' Shop	12	Handker'fs Hemstitched	35
" Cook	1	Jackets, Girls Eaton	3
" Checked	17	Mats Crocheted	10
" White	33	Scarfs, bureau	11
" Waiters	3	Napkins	40
Bodies, drawers	15	Pants	23
Bonnets	18	Pillows	22
Caps, Boys'	13	Quilts	20
" Girls'	5	Sacques, Crochet	1
Cases, Pillow	100	Sheets	129
Cloths, Bread	3	Shirts, Dress	11
Cloths, Dish	21	" Under	15
Table	31	Splashers	3
Wash	19	Spreads	107
Covers, Book	52	Suits	2
Corset	6	Throws	2

GIRLS' EXHIBIT, TERM 1894-95.—CONTINUED.

" Pitcher	17	Tides, Chair	7
" Table	5	Ties, Neck	3
Curtains, prs	18	Towels, Cup	47
Cushions, Chair	5	" Foot	6
Doilies	6	" Hand	79
Drawers, Boys'	11	" Kitchen	1
" Girls'	53	Trimming, crochet	15
Dresses	82	Trimming, Knit	7
Dresses Altered	25	Vests, Girls' under	22
Fascinators	15	Waists, Boys' Shirt	36
Gowns, night	9	Girls' Shirt Waists	69
Handker'fs, plain hemmed	67	Wrappers, Dressing	6

GIRLS' EXHIBIT, TERM 1895-96.

Aprons, Checked dish	30	Gowns, Girls	18
" Eating	12	" Boys	3
" Long Sleeve checked	45	Handkerchiefs	249
" Waiters	4	Mats, Crochet	21
" White	27	" Net woven	56
Bonnets	10	Napkins	76
Cloths, Table	13	Pants	57
" Bread	2	Pillow cases	12
" Butter	6	Quilts	8
" Dish	26	Rugs Hemmed	12
" Tray	12	Scarfs Drawn work	5
" Wash	19	Screens	2
Coats	3	Sheets	108
Comforts	2	Shirts	18
Covers, Corset	6	" Waists, Boys	69
" Table	15	" Girls	71
" Sofa	2	Skirts Dress	36
Curtains	15	" Altered	11
Cushions, Chair	9	Towels, Cup	37
2 Pin	3	" Roller	26
Drawers, Boys	6	Undershirts, Canton flannel	16
" Boys canton flannel	32	Underskirts, Flannel	18
" Girls	30	" White	13
Dresses	110	Under waists, Girls	9
Dresses Altered	25	" canton flannel	22
Fascinators crochet	25	Wrappers	5

IMPROVEMENTS.

During the biennial period embraced in this report, we have torn down the large frame barn that stood just west of the main building, and rebuilt it at a point south of where it formerly stood.

We have also rolled the three-room cottage used as servants' quarters, that formerly stood on our west line near the front of the grounds, to a point south of the main building. These changes have greatly improved the appearance of the premises.

We have built a handsome little reel house of pressed brick to accommodate our fire hose and truck. This has proved a great comfort to us, since our fire hose now stands connected *all the time*. In case of fire, we have only to run with the truck and turn on the water. The building is ornamental as well as useful.

We have also built a neat milk dairy and churning room, just in rear of the kitchen. This is built of pressed brick, and is substantial and ornamental.

The roofs of all the buildings have been overhauled and repaired. All gutters and downspouts repaired and renewed where necessary. A great deal of painting, both inside and outside has been done. Many other smaller items of repairs might be mentioned.

These improvements have been made out of a small surplus saved from our maintenance fund by the most rigid economy.

In this connection, I desire to say that we have improvements and repairs now under way that will consume any surplus that may appear to be accumulated in the hands of the Treasurer.

IMPROVEMENTS NEEDED.

Under this caption I cannot do more than quote from my last report. We have had none of the needs supplied, to which I then called your attention. I will only add that these needs are more pressing now than they were at that time, because of an increased attendance, and on account of others that desire to come:—

We need more shop room; we need a place where our cabinet workmen can finish their work, oiling, varnishing and painting manufactured articles. At present, we have no place where this work can be done.

We also want to add shoe-making to our trades. We have a number of pupils who would be glad to learn this trade. The expense of fitting up a shop would not be great when we get a suitable room for it.

We also need very much, a place to store coal, at present our winter's supply lies out of doors. It is well known that coal exposed to the rain and cold, will slack and deteriorate. It is also open to the depredations of thieves.

We also need a place where a stock of dry lumber can be kept for use in the cabinet shop.

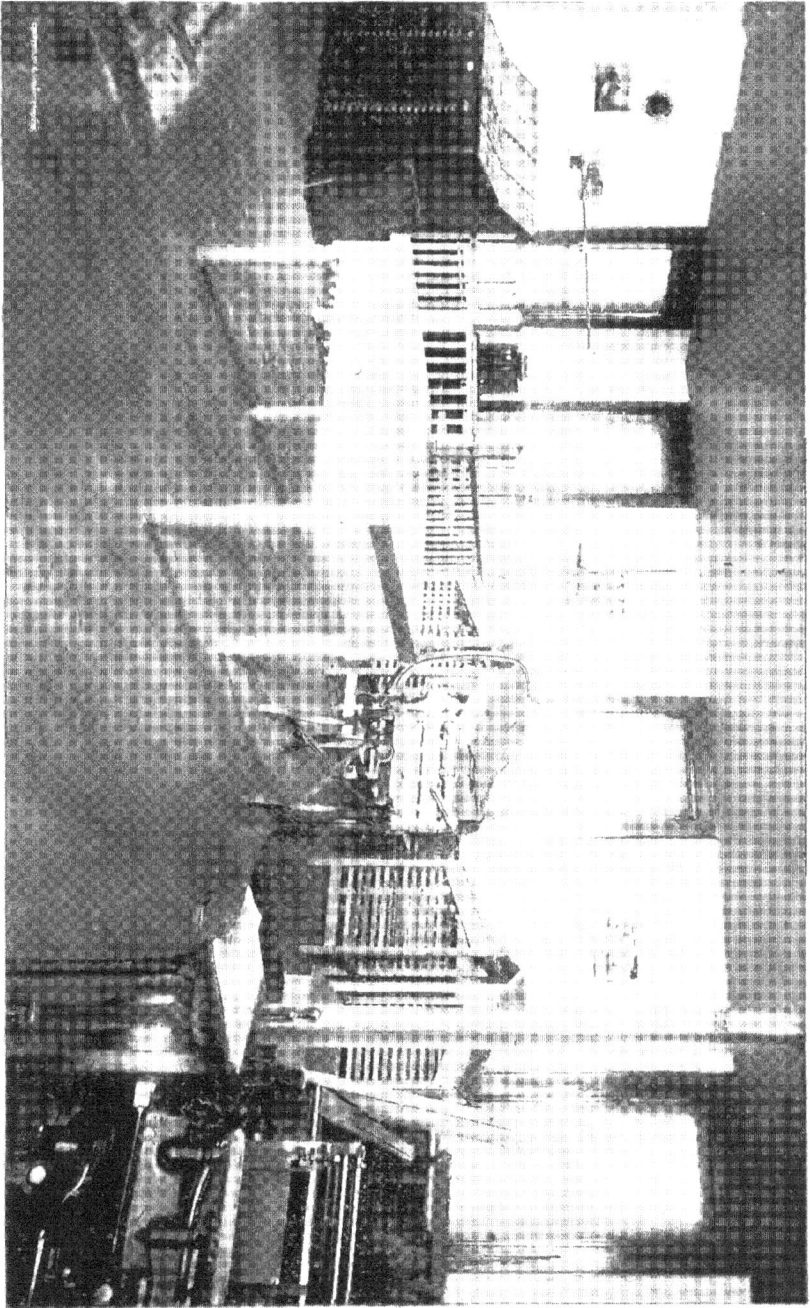

PRINTING OFFICE, ALABAMA INSTITUTE FOR THE DEAF.

We need an ironing room, as our laundry-room is too small, it is very much crowded, and extremely hot and uncomfortable.

We estimate that we can erect a building, an addition or annex to our present shop building, at a cost of about four thousand dollars that will answer for all of these purposes.

We sincerely hope that your Honorable body will see proper to ask the Legislature for an appropriation to erect this building.

Our school-rooms are too small for health and comfort. We wish to throw six of our class rooms into four; we shall then need six other rooms. I think an addition can be made to our present school-building at a comparatively small cost; it is my purpose to make plans and estimates and submit them to your honorable body and ask you to provide us with the additional rooms.

We feel the need, as I have before mentioned, of a gymnasium for the physical development of our children, but this we can wait for until our other wants, which are more pressing, are supplied; we hope however, that you will not lose sight of our needs and our desire to be abreast of our sister institutions in other states, many of which have splendid gymnasiums, of which they are very proud, and whose value they say it is impossible to overestimate.

There are a number of smaller improvements that we need, that we hope to make as soon as we have the time, and as we find we can afford them out of such funds as we can by careful economy save out of our per capita allowance. We will make no mention of these in our report.

FEEBLE-MINDED CHILDREN.

I feel that I cannot close this report without calling your attention to a class of unfortunate children in our State who, of all other children need sympathy and help.

There are in this State, in every county, and in every community, many children who are more helpless and dependent than even the deaf and blind under our care. There is no provision made for these in Alabama. It may seem that I am going out of my proper field of action, and that there is no place in this report for such an appeal as I am about to make. I can only let the cause for which I speak plead my excuses.

There have been a number of these poor feeble-minded children, who have also defective hearing, brought to our doors. Some of these have been admitted; others have been turned away. Those have been admitted who showed the least promise of being benefitted by the methods and plans pursued in the instruction of our pupils. The others were turned away, not because they could not be instructed or benefitted, but because we could not do so with our plans and methods. They could not take their places in our classes, with even the dullest of our pupils, but would require special methods and more or less individual attention that we are not prepared to give. We cannot do this for them, because we have not sufficient funds to employ the necessary instructors, and help, to care for them.

I can to-day name and locate enough of these feeble-minded children who have been denied admittance here to form a full class for more than one instructor, and I know that there are many others.

It is the duty of somebody to take the initiative in a movement to provide for this class of the State's unfortunate children.

I know of no body of persons more competent by reason of ability to inaugurate such a movement; or possessed of more interest in unfortunate humanity that this honorable board.

I suggest that the feeble-minded *deaf* at least might, be provided for in connection with this Institution, and possibly it might be the part of the wisdom to include all classes of feeble-minded children in this one movement, until the number brought together made it necessary, or advisable to establish a separate institution in this or some other community.

This subject has been brought home to me so often in the past few years, and I am so much impressed with the necessity and the justice of it, that I deemed it my duty to officially bring the matter to your attention, with the hope that you can, and will take steps to secure the needed provision for these poor little ones.

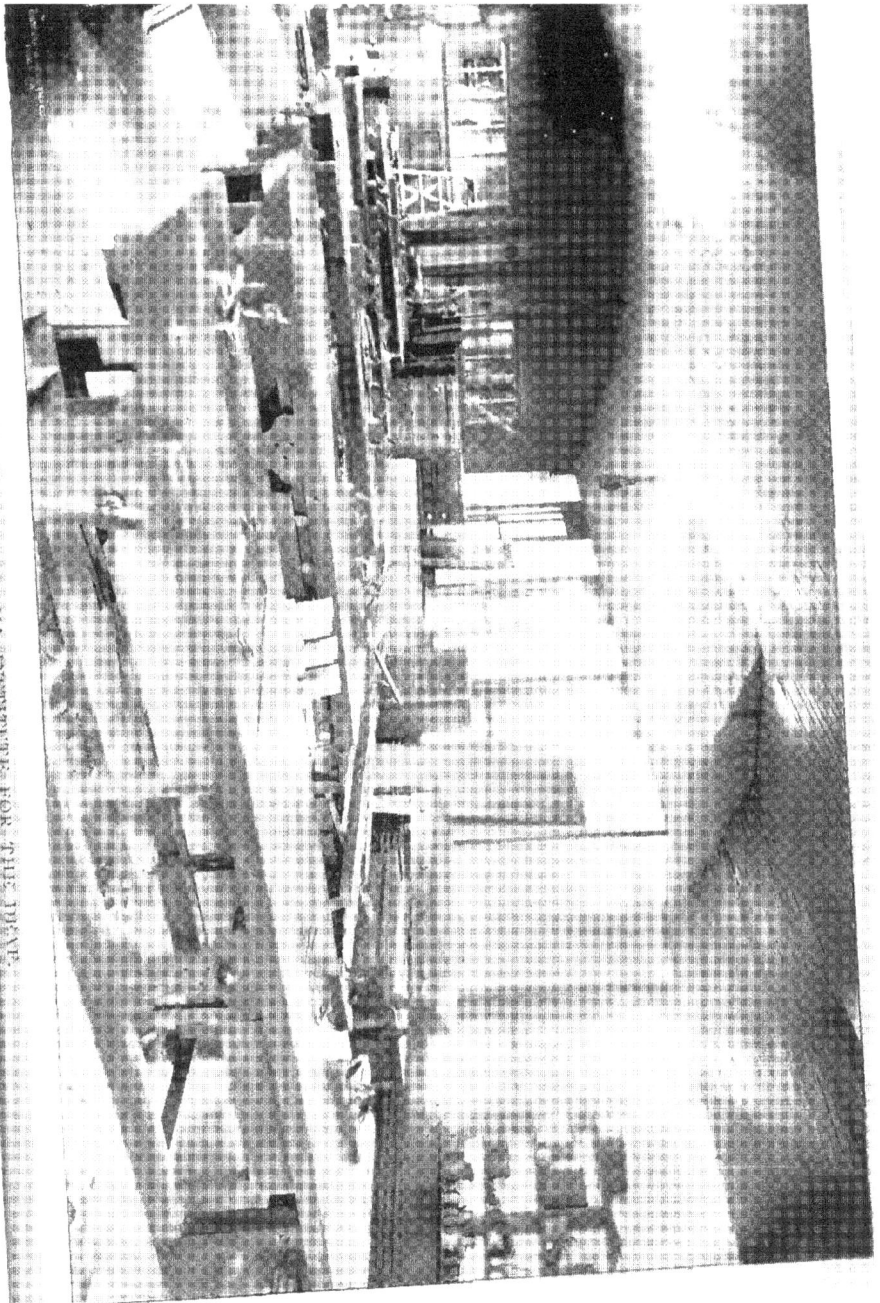

ALABAMA ACADEMY FOR THE BLIND.

ATTENDANCE.

We have enrolled one hundred and four pupils: fifty-five boys and forty-nine girls. Forty counties are represented; twenty-six counties are not represented. The pupils present are distributed among the counties represented as follows:

Bibb	2	Lauderdale	3
Blount	1	Lawrence	1
Bullock	1	Lee	4
Calhoun	5	Limestone	5
Chambers	5	Madison	3
Choctaw	1	Marion	1
Clay	2	Marshall	3
Clarke	3	Mobile	4
Coffee	1	Monroe	2
Colbert	2	Montgomery	1
Crenshaw	1	Morgan	2
Dale	3	Randolph	2
Dekalb	3	Russell	1
Elmore	2	Shelby	2
Fayette	3	St. Clair	1
Geneva	1	Talladega	5
Henry	4	Tallapoosa	4
Jackson	7	Tuscaloosa	3
Jefferson	10	Walker	1
Lamar	1	Winston	1

Total 104.

HEALTH.

We have no serious illness of any kind to record. No deaths; no epidemic since last report. One case of chronic trouble, two light cases of pneumonia, and two cases of measles, are the only instances of sickness worthy of note.

We are still without sanitary sewer connection. This we deem necessary for perfect safety in the matter of health. I have had made a profile and estimate of the cost of construction of a line of a sewer that will connect us with the sewerage system of the city. It can be completed for twelve hundred dollars, and I respectfully represent that it ought to be done as soon as possible. I have no doubt of your ability to obtain an appropriation from the Legislature for that purpose.

STAFF.

At the close of the term of 1894-95, the Resident Superintendent, the Matron, and two Teachers resigned. The Superintendent, Professor Mitchell left us to take up the study of medicine; the Matron, desiring a year's rest, was not a candidate for reappointment. The two Teachers, the Misses Hemphill resigned; they have since engaged in teaching in Tuscaloosa, Ala.

Prof. F. H. Manning, late of the Colorado School for the Blind, was appointed Resident Superintendent. Mrs. F. H. Manning was appointed Matron. They began work in August 1895.

At the beginning of the term in September 1895, Miss A. W. Brockman and Miss Lilah McDaniel, both of this State, were appointed teachers. Later Miss F. I. Leonard, of Boston, Mass., was engaged in the literary department, and Mr. Thomas L. Williams of this city, in the musical department.

LITERARY DEPARTMENT.

As will be seen by reference to the table below, the curriculum at the Academy covers all the ground of the grammar and high school work of our city schools. Graduates from this school, with the exception of the *Languages*, would be prepared to enter the sophomore class, in the classical course, at the State University.

The following is a list of the subjects taught in this department, the past two years, and the number of of students instructed in each:

Arithmetic	77	English Grammar	18
Algebra	16	Lessons in English	28
Geometry	4	Elementary Science	11
Spelling	56	Botany	7
Geography	71	Hygiene and Physiology	36
United States History	30	Civil Government	5
General History	5	Political Economy	4
Reading	56	Current News	104

Additions have been made from time to time to the stock of

ALABAMA ACADEMY FOR THE BLIND.

apparatus specially adapted to the instruction of the blind. It is our policy to provide everything that our means will allow in the way of tangible apparatus that will aid the pupils in the pursuit of their studies, and in the acquisition of knowledge.

We stress the importance of having all the classes practice reading, both point and line type, as a daily exercise, with the view of becoming expert at reading by touch, hoping by this means to form in the individual pupil the habit of independent reading. To further encourage the reading habit, we frequently purchase new and attractive books in raised type for the pupils' library.

For the profit and entertainment of the pupils, the teachers in the literary department have organized reading classes, to each of which, standard books and magazine articles are read.

The pupils enjoy these readings greatly, and no work done in school is more profitable or beneficial. This will be readily understood, when it is known that the supply of literature for the blind in raised type is limited to a few hundred volumes. These readings open to them the vast fields of science, fiction and general literature.

MUSICAL DEPARTMENT.

We have employed an additional instructor in this department since the date of our last report, in the person of Mr. Thomas L. Williams. We are not as well equipped as we would like to be; we need several new instruments that we cannot now afford; but we believe that we are doing as good work as any similar institution of the same size and equipment.

We are especially anxious to have a pipe organ. The best work cannot be done without this instrument. We trust that the Legislature will provide for this need at an early day. We have the necessary instruments for an excellent orchestra and brass band.

The number of pupils instructed in the different branches of musical work the past two years is as follows:

Chorus	104	Band	14
Piano	45	Cornet	15
Organ	19	Piccolo	3
Theory of Music	20	Orchestra	15
Tuning	10	Violin	14

INDUSTRIAL DEPARTMENT.

A short time before our last report, we began instruction in piano tuning, and repairing. This work has been conducted on rather a limited scale, but the results have been good. Several of our boys have become expert at tuning and can make any ordinary repairs upon piano or organ. We wish very much to do more in this direction, and we expect to bend our energies toward this end. We cannot expect to accomplish a great deal until we have more work room, and more means to supply a more extensive equipment than we can now afford.

The mattress and cane shops continue to do good work, many of our boys are expert at cane seating, and mattress making That the boys have worked well, is evidenced by the following list of articles turned out from the shops:

Mattresses made	92	Door mats made	23
Chairs seated	567	Horse Collars made	22

The number of boys under instruction at the different kinds of work, is as follows:

Cane seating	40	Mat making	10
Mattress making	20	Tuning and Repairing	10
Collar making	10		

The girls are taught plain and and fancy needle-work, and how to use the sewing machine, plain knitting, lace knitting, crocheting and bead work. The following list of articles were made by the girls during the term of 1895-96:

Handkerchiefs and towels	100	Aprons	13
Sheets	17	Bibs	39
Pillow cases	23	Under garments	8

In bead work there made numerous articles of various kinds.

It is proper to note that the average time given to shop work for boys was five hours per week, and for girls, two hours per week

PHYSICAL CULTURE.

Two years ago I called your attention to this feature of our work in following language:—

"The value of physical training within proper limits, as an aid to mental development, is too well established to admit of question

What is true of our hearing and sighted young people in our universities and colleges is doubly true in the case of the defective classes committed to our care, and with no class of defective children is this need so keenly felt as with the blind.

Ths experience of our more fortunate sister institutions which possess well equipped gymnasiums impels us to appeal strongly and with confidence to your honorable body for material encouragement to hope for an early realization of our desires along this line.

We feel sure that if the members of the Legislature could be made to appreciate the value of systematic, scientific exercise for our blind children, they would not withhold it from us a day longer than they felt that the State could afford to provide it for them."

This need remains unsupplied; but to meet the necessities of the situation, as nearly as possible, we have further extended our system of drills with dumb-bells, clubs, and wands with gratifying results, demonstrating what a great boon a well-equipped gymnasium would be.

IMPROVEMENTS AND REPAIRS.

In the spring of 1895, all of the gutters on all of the buildings were over-hauled and repaired or replaced with new gutters. On two of the buildings, as originally constructed, the gutters lay on the walls, and were subject to overflow, and in case of a leak the water ran down on the walls. These gutters have been made to overhang the walls, new and larger down spouts supplied, and now all the water is easily carried off and the walls protected.

In the winter of 1895-96, the steam boiler which has been in use since 1889 gave out and the purchase of a new boiler became a necessity. This boiler has been bought and placed in position at a total cost of about eight hundred dollars. An elevator shaft and elevator has also been constructed to get coal into the boiler room and to remove ashes, etc., from same.

The cost of the boiler, elevator, etc., was paid out of our maintenance fund, and it has caused us to anticipate our revenues to that extent.

IMPROVEMENTS NEEDED.

We have sixty-three pupils on our roll today; there are others to come. About seventy is as many as we can comfortably accomodate. We have made no effort to increase our numbers, because we did not want to overcrowd our buildings.

For about four thousand dollars we can build a house that will increase our dormitory capacity nearly fifty per cent. For six thousand dollars additional, we can erect a building that will give us all the room we need, for every purpose, and increase our capacity fully one hundred per cent. We need a neat substantial fence around the entire property. The present fence is one built in 1886, when the property was first purchased, is made of pine boards and posts, and has about given out.

I have already called your attention to the need of sewer connection.

INSTITUTION OCULISTS.

For a number of years, prior to 1895, Drs. Baldwin and Thigpen gave us their services gratuitously. The school having increased in number, and the work becoming quite laborious, the Board thought proper to ask these gentlemen to accept some remuneration for their services. Accordingly in June 1895 Drs. Baldwin and Thigpen were officially selected as our oculists, and they are paid the nominal sum of twenty-five dollars per day for their services. The Board ordered that the oculists visit the Institution at least twice each term, in November, and in April.

The past two years, Dr. Thigpen has given his attention to this work, making us several visits. He has examined every pupil, and a record of the case, noting the history, cause, and method of treatment has been recorded.

A number of operations have been performed with more or less success in every case.

CLASS ROOM ALABAMA ACADEMY FOR THE BLIND.

ALABAMA SCHOOL FOR NEGRO DEAF-MUTES AND BLIND.

ATTENDANCE.

We have enrolled in this school during the Biennial period seventy-two pupils, forty-six boys and twenty-six girls.

They are divided as to classes, i. e. deaf and blind, and as to sex as follows:

DEAF.

Boys	19	Girls	14

Total 33.

BLIND.

Boys	27	Girls	12

Total 39.

Numbers in attendance, September 30th, 1896.

DEAF.

Boys	12	Girls	11

Total 23.

BLIND.

Boys	20	Girls	7

Total 27.

Twenty-five counties are represented as follows:

Bibb	5	Limestone	2
Bullock	1	Lowndes	1
Calhoun	1	Macon	6
Clay	1	Montgomery	6
Chambers	2	Morgan	3
Colbert	2	Perry	1
Dallas	1	Pickens	1
Etowah	1	St. Clair	1
Escambia	1	Sumpter	1
Greene	2	Talladega	15
Jefferson	13	Tuscaloosa	1
Lawrence	1	Wilcox	1
Lauderdale	2		

Total 72.

LITERARY DEPARTMENT

In this department only the primary branches are taught, such as Reading, Writing, Spelling, Arithmetic, Geography, Elementary Grammar and Composition

MUSICAL DEPARTMENT

In this department vocal and instrumental music are taught; instruction is given to a few of the most talented on the organ, violin and cornet.

INDUSTRIAL DEPARTMENT.

This is decidedly the most important department of our school, for all of our pupils after leaving school must depend upon manual labor for their support. The following trades are taught: Carpentering, Upholstering, Cane Seating, Basket making, and Gardening. The girls are taught Sewing, Cooking, Laundry work and House work.

GIRLS' EXHIBIT.

Clothes, Table	6	Shirt waists, girls	12
Napkins	102	Drawers	140
Towels, Bath	192	" Bodies	6
" Cup	96	Dresses	98
Sheets	165	Gowns	12
Cases, Pillow	173	Chemise	13
Ticks, Bed	21	Undershirts,	38
Aprons	51	Pants	101
Handkerchiefs	68	Curtains	6
Shirt waists	681	Chairs Seated	94

BOYS' EXHIBIT

Chairs seated	2	Wagon beds	2
Mattresses	21	Arithmetical Slates	12
Clothes Chests	1	Cistern Tops	2
Wardrobes	5	Hoe Handles	15
Bins for Pantry	3	Tables	3
Cupboards	2	Work Benches	8
Ladders	2	Baskets	33
Benches	8	Cisterns	2
Map Cases	1	Cess Pools	1
Desk	1	Plank Fencing	3070 ft.
Flower Stands	1	Wire "	900 "
Rocking Chairs	2	Square yards sodding	1900 "
Wash benches	3	Macadamized drives	340 "
Drying racks	3	Water Pipe laid	320 "
Hat Rack	1	Tile Drainage	85 "

IMPROVEMENTS.

In the fall of 1894 we erected a two-room frame building, for

a laundry, and in the fall of 1895, a two-room frame building for a shop. Each of these buildings is valued at one thousand dollars. The work was almost all done by the pupils of the school, and the cost of each building did not exceed five hundred dollars.

A cow barn, valued at about three hundred dollars, has also been built; the work being done by the pupils. A milk dairy and a flower pit are also among the improvements during the past two years.

In the summer of 1895 the south end of the main building was raised from one and a half to two and a half stories, giving us three large rooms, where we formerly had one small room.

This change added twenty-five per cent. to the capacity of our girls dormitories; it also added greatly to the appearance of the building. The cost of this improvement was about eight hundred dollars.

Acting under instructions from the Board seven acres of land lying east and south of our grounds, have been purchased. We now have fifteen acres of land, the shape of the entire lot being a parallelogram; three acres wide, and five acres deep. The cost of the seven acres purchased last was two hundred and forty dollars. This land was needed, and added greatly to the convenience and value of the property. The cost of all of the improvements made, has come out of our maintenance fund.

We have been able to do this only by the closest economy.

HEALTH.

With but few exceptions, the health of the pupils has been good. I regret to report the death of two pupils. James Gardener, a blind boy from Jefferson County who died on the 22nd, of October, 1895, of pneumonia, and Douglass Meadows, a deaf boy from Chambers County, who died very suddenly on December 1st, 1895, of apoplexy.

During the spring of 1896, we had an epidemic of measles, seventeen cases in all, but without serious results.

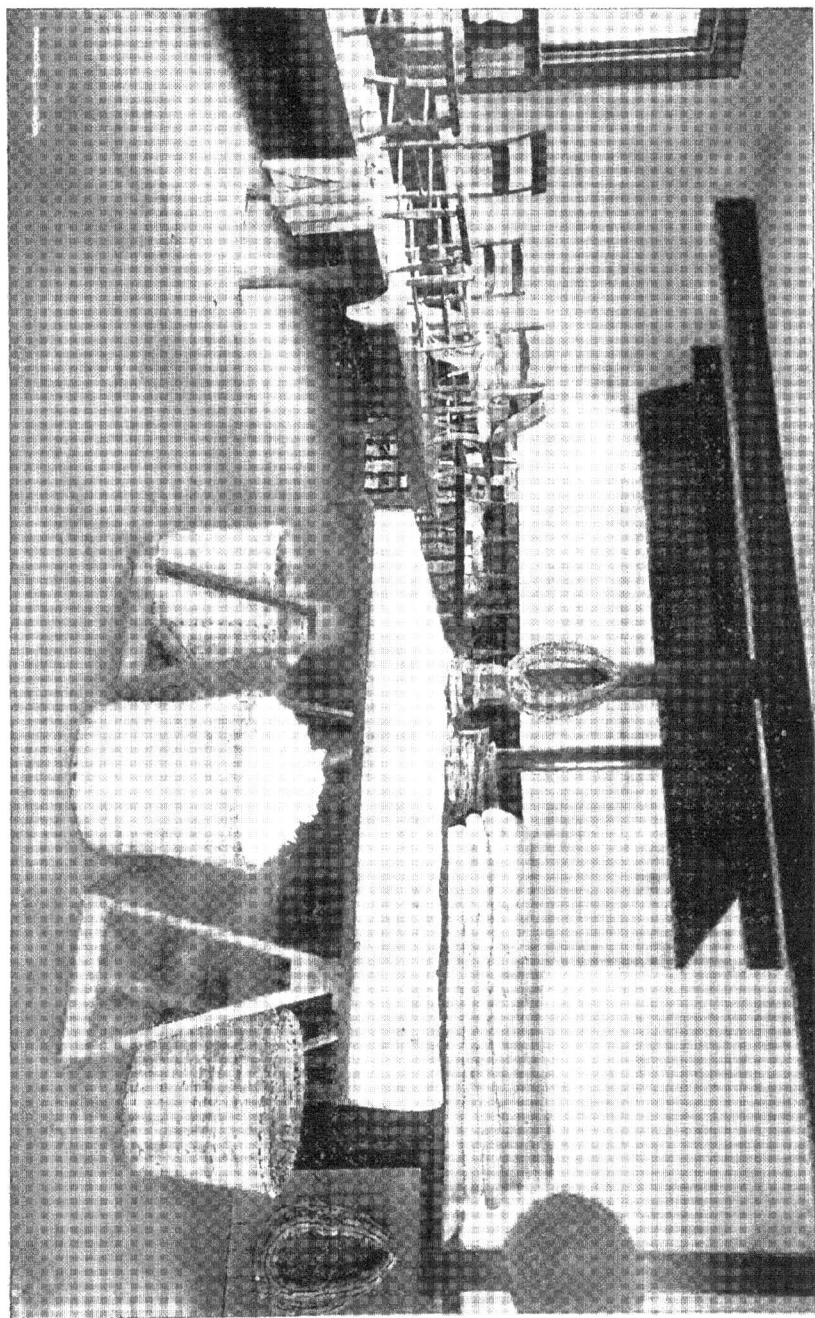

INSURANCE.

The total amount of insurance upon the property of the State is $88,050.00, distributed as follows:

Upon the buildings and their contents, at the Institution for the Deaf, $50,000.00. At the Academy for the Blind, $27,800.00. And at the school for Negro Deaf-Mutes and Blind, $10,250.00. In all cases we have taken out three-year policies, thereby getting three years' insurance for two annual premiums.

The insurance is distributed among twelve or more strong companies. And the policies are kept in a fire-proof safe in the office of the Secretary of the Board.

ALABAMA SCHOOL FOR NEGRO DEAF MUTES AND BLIND

ACKNOWLEDGMENTS.

Acting under instructions from the Board, I have had the words, "Wilson Shops" placed in raised stone letters over the front entrance to our industrial building, in honor of John Wilson, Esq., of Pike Roads, Montgomery County, Ala., who left us the first and only legacy that the Institution has ever received. The proceeds of which were spent in building and equipping this department.

We wish to tender our thanks and express our appreciation of the favors shown us by the obliging local officials of all the railroads that run into Talladega, for valuable assistance and for their uniform kindness in receiving and sending away pupils, handling baggage, etc.

We also desire to express our thanks to all the railroad companies who have generously granted us reduced rates and special favors from time to time.

We wish to tender our special thanks to the Louisville & Nashville R. R. Co., to Mr. Milton H. Smith and Supt. Knox for an annual pass between points in Alabama, and also to the Southern R. R. Company, and G. P. A., W. A. Turk for passes over the Southern and controlled lines in Alabama, enabling us to reach many unfortunate deaf and blind children, whom we could not have otherwise reached.

We give below a list of newspapers that are sent to the Institution free of charge. To each and every one of these we wish to express our grateful appreciation:

The Daily Advertiser	Montgomery, Ala.
Deaf-Mute Advance	Jacksonville, Ill.
The Maryland Bulletin	Frederick, Md.
The Banner	Devils Lake, N. Dak.
Buff and Blue	Washington, D. C.
The Alabama Baptist	Montgomery, Ala.
The Companion	Faribault, Minn.
The Ohio Chronicle	Columbus, Ohio.
The Canadian Mute	Belleville, Canada.
State-Herald	Birmingham, Ala.
The Kentucky Standard	Danville, Ky.
The Silent Echo	Winnepeg, Manitoba.
The Deseret Eagle	Ogden, Utah.

34

Our Dumb Animals .... Boston, Mass.
The Goodson Gazette .... Staunton, Va.
The Deaf-Mute Hawkeye............... Council Bluff, Iowa.
Colorado Index .... Colorado Springs, Col
The Mentor............................. Malone, N. Y.
The Mirror .... Eutaw, Ala.
The Journal .... Tuskaloosa, Ala.
Bulletin of Correction & Charities...... St. Paul, Minn.
The Institution News................... Austin, Texas.
Our Mountain Home.... .... Talladega, Ala.
The Silent Hoosier.................... Indianapolis, Ind.
The Deaf-Mute Journal ....New York, N. Y.
The Atlanta Journal.................... Atlanta, Ga
The Michigan Mirror.................... Flint, Mich
Nebraska Journal....... .... Omaha, Neb.
The Mentor.... .... Boston, Mass.
The Weekly News ... . Berkley, Cal.
The Institute Herald .... St. Augustine, Fla
The Optic....... .... Little Rock, Ark.
The Silent Observer .... Knoxville, Tenn.
Daily Paper For Our Little Folks....... Rochester, N. Y.
Wilcox Progress. .... Camden, Ala.
The Palmetto Leaf. ....Cedar Spring, S. C.
The Pelican .... Baton Rouge, La.
The Western Pennsylvanian .... Edgewood, Pa.
The Deaf-Mute Register ... . Rome, N. Y.
The LaFayette Sun .... LaFayette, Ala.
The Sign .... Salem, Oregon.
The Kansas Star .... Olathe, Kan.
The Shelby Sentinel.................... Calera, Ala.
The Tablet .... Romney W. Va.
The Wisconsin Times .... Delavan, Wis.
The Washingtonian . ... Vancouver, Was
The Mt. Airy World .... Mt. Airy, Pa.
The Lone Star Weekly............... Austin, Texas.
The Deaf-Mute Voice.... .... Jackson, Miss.
The Silent Worker.. ....Trenton, N. J.
What Cheer. .... Providence, R. I.
The Kelly Messenger ... . Morganton, N. C.
Glen Mills Daily...... .... Glen Mills, Pa.
The News-Reporter.................... Talladega, Ala.
The Herald .... Union Springs, Ala.
The Advertiser .... New Decatur, Ala.
Ephphatha............................ London, England.
The Silent Messenger................. Belfast, Ireland.
The British Deaf-Mute............. ... Bolton, England.
The Deaf & Dumb .... Derby, England.
The Idea.... .... Jacksonville, Ill.
The Brundidge News .... Brundidge, Ala.

Very respectfully,

J. H. JOHNSON,

Principal.

A MEMORIAL TRIBUTE TO THE CHARACTER AND WORTH OF HON. SAMUEL K. McSPADDEN.

Your committee appointed at the recent annual meeting of our Board of Trustees to prepare resolutions and memorial tribute to the worth and character of the late Hon. Samuel K. McSpadden, beg leave to report as follows:

RESOLVED, That in the death of Chancellor McSpadden, late a fellow trustee, this Board is deeply moved and extends to the family of the deceased, to the State of Alabama, to the state judiciary and to the battle-scarred Confederate veterans sincere condolence in their loss and bereavement.

RESOLVED, That in the death of Chancellor McSpadden the country has sustained a loss which has been felt and deplored in all parts of the Commonwealth.

RESOLVED, That the Board communicate these resolutions, with the accompanying tribute, to the family of the deceased, to the State Executive, and that the same be spread on the records of this Institute.

Samuel King McSpadden was born in Warren County, Tennessee, November 12, 1823. He was the son of the Rev. Samuel McSpadden, one of the founders and early ministers of the Cumberland Presbyterian Church. His mother was Miss Rebecca Donaldson, a native of South Carolina.

Of the surroundings of the son's childhood and early life little is known to your committee. It is however learned that his educational advantages were limited—that he had no opportunity of reaping the benefit of collegiate instruction and that he was a stranger to the curriculum of the University. But far above college ethics, he received a priceless training in morals and all the higher virtues from a devoted Christian mother, from whose precepts and admonitions he never departed. From an exemplary father, limited in facilities, means, time and opportunity for imparting instruction, he was inspired with a love of history, biography and general literature which gave him that thirst for knowledge for which he was noted. With such precepts and examples as a basis, he began the battle of life. To a great extent he was self educated, and almost wholly self-made. He was of Scotch-Irish stock, a race noted for self-reliance, pluck and energy, and distinguished in the history of our country for the leaders of renown that it has furnished: unpretentious in demeanor, his mind was active in all the fields of human activities. Self-reliance was a leading attribute of the Chancellor's character, supplemented by industry, pluck, energy and a conscientious discharge of duty.

Leaving the old homestead at the age of nineteen, skilled in the art of saddle and harness making which he acquired at Winchester, Tenn., he came to Talladega in the year 1842, and here, for about seven years as a journeyman, plied his chosen trade—the work of his handicraft always giving high satisfaction. Meanwhile under a quiet and unpretentious demeanor, fired with the ambition to explore a field more congenial to his taste, with the hope and promise of moving on a higher plane of life, and thus while industriously using the implements of the saddler as his daily vocation, he was likewise diligently devoting every spare moment to the assimilation of Coke and Blackstone. His modesty, his high moral worth, combined with uniform courtesy and gentleness of manner, won for him the aid, encouragement, respect and esteem of the entire bar of Talladega of which McConnell, the elder Bowden, Stone, Rice, Chilton, Morgan Bowie, Parsons, White, Curry, Cruikshanks and others scarcely less distinguished were members. In evidence of the ability of this bar, it is only necessary to recall the fact that three of the members were subsequently elevated to the supreme court bench of Alabama, one became governor of the State, four of them were representatives in the United States Congress, two became members of the Confederate States Congress, while one now holds the exalted position of Alabama's senior representative in the United States Senate; and doubtless the noble presence of this brilliant bar may have had much to do at this period in shaping the future course of our late associate. Finally completing his course of law in the office of the late Hon. Saml. F. Rice, he was licensed and began the practice of his newly acquired profession, in 1850, at Centre, Cherokee County, Alabama. Here he located and was rewarded with a liberal, if not lucrative practice, and by frugality and careful management amassed a handsome property.

The Chancellor was happily united in marriage at Centre, Ala., June 11th, 1854, to Miss Charlotte Ann Garrett, the handsome and cultured daughter of Gen. John H. Garrett. The issue of this union was one child, Lula, now the wife of Hon. H. W. Cardeu, of Centre.

For half a century Chancellor McSpadden was a member in high standing in the Masonic Order. Both he and Mrs. McSpadden were members of the Presbyterian Church.

Patriotism was a leading trait of the Chancellor's character. He was devoted to his adopted State and his native South. The war between the States becoming a reality in 1861, we find him, at an early day, leaving the peaceful pursuits of civil life and enlisting in the armies of the Confederacy. In espousing that cause he joined the 19th Alabama Regiment and soon became its Colonel. Through the perils and privations of camp and the strife, conflict and carnage of battle he continued in command of this regiment of gallant Alabama troops from Shiloh to Resaca. At Resaca, May, 1864, he fell into the hands of the Federals and was taken to Johnson's Island where he was retained until March, 1865, and never again joined his command.

As a legislator our late associate represented his people in the State senate for a number of terms with a wise and faithful and fearless discharge of duty to his constituency—and always receiving the plaudits "well done, thou good and faithful servant."

For many years he was the popular, upright, impartial, fearless and efficient Chancellor of the Northeastern Division of Alabama. In the discharge of his official duties he gave very general satisfaction to all classes of litigants coming before his court. As a matter of fact, the decisions of no judicial officer were so rarely reversed as his.

We come now to remark on the Chancellor's connection with our body as a trustee of this Institute. For while the writer of this brief tribute has had the good fortune to have known him intimately and enjoyed his confidence since his first appearance in Talladega "in the long ago," it was as a member of the Board that most of us came to know him well, and to admire his sterling qualities of mind and heart. Having been just appointed in 1884 by Governor O'Neal to fill the vacancy in the Board resulting from the death of Hon. G. T. McAfee, he promptly accepted service, and at once became a most valued member. He was seldom absent from any of our imporant meetings when it was possible to be present. He was an earnest, wise and efficient co-laborer and ever ready to aid in all work looking to the benefit of the Institute in all its departments. While always careful of the interests of the state, he never allowed any false economy to mar, or interrupt the substantial progress and efficiency of the Institute.

The great dominant force of Chancellor McSpadden, was his high and inflexible christian morality. For mental ability, however great and varied, avails little without the basis of moral force. If he lacked genius, he possessed what is better, judgement. He made no pretense to those mental qualities which dazzle and astonish mankind, but he had a discretion which seldom committed a mistake; an integrity that always looked to duty—a will that never swerved from his purpose, a diligence that mastered any subject, and a perseverence that yielded to nothing but the impossible. His personal quaities were of the highest order, urbane, cordial and graceful in manners, and congenial adaptability, with a voice low, soft and confiding, he never failed to awaken interest and confidence in those with whom he came in contact.

We shall not dwell upon the end. Chancellor McSpadden passed away in the ripeness of knowledge and the Psalmist's allotted fullness of years, at his home at Centre, May 3, 1896. He continued in the discharge of the active duties of life until within a few weeks of his death. His character was truly a blending of all the better qualities of our nature :

> "And the elements,
> So mixed in him, that Nature might stand up,
> And say to all the world : *"This was a man"*

WM. TAYLOR,
W. H. BURR,
G. A. JOINER,
J. B. McMILLAN.

TREASURER'S REPORT.

J. B. McMILLAN, Treasurer,
    In Account with The Alabama Institution for the Deaf,
        The Alabama Academy for the Blind,
        Ala. School for the Negro D. M. & B.

INSURANCE AND REPAIR FUND.

For the two fiscal years ending Sept. 30th, 1896.

1894		
Sept. 29	To balance on hand	$ 22 61
Oct. 3	To cash from State Treasurer	500 00
" 29	" " "	500 00
1895		
Oct. 9	" " "	1,000 00
	Total	$2,022 61

CR

1895		
Apr. 6	By cash paid Carleton Mitchell, Superintendent	$ 250 00
June 11	" " W. T. Thornton, Agent	343 00
" 14	" " McConnell & Boynton, Agent	60 00
" 17	" " Dillon & Storey	171 00
1896		
Jan. 10	" " J. H. Johnson, Principal	281 90
	Total	$1,105 90
	To balance on hand	$ 916 71

TREASURER'S ACCOUNT.

J. B. McMILLAN, Treasurer:

In Account with The Alabama Institute for the Deaf,
The Alabama Academy for the Blind,
Ala. School for the Negro D. M. & B.

For the two fiscal years ending Sept. 30th, 1896.

Date	Description	Amount
1894		
Sept. 29	To Balance.	$ 1,897 86
	Cash Rebate on clothing	33 25
	" " "	72 78
Oct. 3	From State Treasurer	5,946 56
17	" Shops	10 00
29	" State Treasurer	5,946 56
Dec. 13	Rebate on clothing	40 82
21	From shops	5 00
1895		
Jan. 8	Rebate on clothing	118 00
10	From shops	24 00
	State Treasurer	13,261 87
Mar. 15	Rebate on clothing	12 50
30	From shops . .	76 58
Apr. 3	State Treasurer	12,706 87
May. 13	Rebate on clothing	57 55
June. 26	From Printing Office	23 17
July. 2	State Treasurer	12,686 87
Aug. 3	Shops and clothing	44 63
29	Rebate on clothing	23 40
	" " "	13 80
	" " " .	28 65
Sept. 7	From Sale of old boiler	40 00
Oct. 9	State Treasurer . . .	13,089 37
Dec. 4	Shops	2 75
1896		
Jan. 6	State Treasurer	13,425 00
Apr 6	" "	13,425 00
May. 9	Shops	5 00
13	Printing Office . .	21 97
July. 3	Sale old Refrigerator	5 00
4	State Treasurer . .	6,712 50
13	" "	6,712 50
Aug. 18	Rebate on clothing and shoes	16 75
	From Cabinet Shops	16 00
Sept. 19	Shops	23 95
24	Sale of old goods, &c.	12 75
	Total	$ 106,539 26

1894		CR.	
Oct.	3	By cash paid Express on papers	25
		J. B. McMillan, Treas	37 50
	6	J. H. Johnson, Prin	2,500 00
		J. H. Johnson, Prin	745 90
		J. H. Johnson	375 00
		Mrs. J. H. Johnson	125 00
		W. S. Johnson	175 00
		Osce Roberts	225 00
		Miss M. McGuire	175 00
		Miss M. Toney	125 00
		Miss A. L. Johnson	200 00
		S. J. Johnson	250 00
		J. S. Graves, Supt	1,000 00
		J. S. Graves, Supt	492 09
		J. S. Graves	200 00
		Mrs. Olla Graves	100 00
		A. F. Wood	150 00
		Carleton Mitchell, Supt	1,500 00
		Carleton Mitchell, Supt	1,107 12
		Carleton Mitchell	500 00
		A. W. Williams	150 00
		Miss M. E. Shugh	125 00
	10	J. S. Laverty	225 00
		J. F. Bledsoe	150 00
		J. H. Johnson, Prin	62 50
		J. H. Johnson, Prin	62 50
Nov.	17	1st Nat. Bank Talladega	95 25
1895			
Jan.	8	Express on Papers	25
	12	Osce Roberts	225 00
		Miss M. McGuire	175 60
		J. H. Johnson	375 00
		J. B. McMillan	37 50
		S. J. Johnson	250 00
		Miss A. L. Johnson	200 00
		A. F. Wood	150 00
		Mrs. Olla Graves	100 00
		J. S. Graves	200 00
		Geo. Thomason	75 00
		J. S. Graves, Supt	1,000 00
		J. S. Graves, Supt	1,534 39
		J. S. Laverty	225 00
		A. W. Williams	150 00
		Miss E. Hemphill	125 00
		Miss C. Hemphill	125 00
		Carleton Mitchell	300 00
		Miss M. E. Shugh	125 00
		Carleton Mitchell, Supt...	1,200 00
	18	Carleton Mitchell, Supt	1,840 50
		J. H. Johnson, Prin	2,500 00
		J. H Johnson, Prin	2,001 93
		T. S. McMoney	60 00
		Miss M. E. Toney	125 00
		Miss S. A. Tillinghast	125 00
		W. S. Johnson	175 00
		J. F. Bledsoe	150 00
Apr.	2	Express on papers	25
	4	J. B. McMillan, Treas	37 50
	6	Carleton Mitchell	300 00

1895					
Apr.	6	By cash paid	Carleton Mitchell, Supt....	$	1,200 00
			Carleton Mitchell, Supt.		1,663 73
			A. W. Williams........		150 00
			Miss C. Hemphill....		125 00
			Miss E. Hemphill..		125 00
			Miss M. E. Shugh		125 00
			J. S. Graves...........		200 00
			J. S. Graves, Supt		1,000 00
			J. S. Graves, Supt		655 51
			Geo. Thomason...		75 00
			Mrs. Olla Graves..		100 00
			J. H. Johnson.		375 00
			J. H. Johnson, Prin....		2,500 00
			J. H. Johnson, Prin		1,323 90
			S. J. Johnson. ...		250 00
			W. S. Johnson		175 00
			T. S. McAloney		150 00
			J. F. Bledsoe.		150 00
			Osee Roberts.....		225 00
			Miss A. L. Johnson.		200 00
			Miss S. A. Tillinghast		125 00
			Miss M. McGuire..		175 00
			Miss M. Toney.		125 00
	13		J. S. Laverty.		225 00
	15		A. F. Wood		150 00
	27		State Treasurer.....		20 00
June.	5		J. H. Johnson, Prin..		1,268 00
	12		Express on papers..		25
July.	25		A. F. Wood		150 00
			Carleton Mitchell, Supt		1,200 00
			Carleton Mitchell, Supt....		1,171 27
			Miss C. Hemphill		250 00
			Miss E. Hemphill...		250 00
	6		Carleton Mitchell.		300 00
			A. W. Williams..		150 00
			Miss M. E. Shugh.		125 00
			J. S. Graves, Supt.		2,000 00
			J. S. Graves, Supt		753 87
			J. S. Graves		200 00
			Mrs. J. S. Graves		100 00
			Geo. Thomason		75 00
	13		J. S. Laverty.		225 00
			Osee Roberts		225 00
			Express on money		9 55
			S. J. Johnson		250 00
			Miss M. McGuire		350 00
			Miss A. L. Johnson		200 00
			J. H. Johnson, Prin		2,500 00
			T. S. McAloney....		195 00
			J. H Johnson		375 00
			J. F. Bledsoe		150 00
			S. A. Tillinghast		125 00
	27		W. S. Johnson		175 00
			Miss M. E. Toney		125 00
Aug.	27		J. B. McMillian Treas		37 50
			Carleton Mitchell		200 00
			J. H. Johnson, Prin.		500 00
			1st Nat. Bank Talladega		89 18
Oct.	8		J H. Johnson, Supt		1,482 37

1895			
Oct.	8	By cash paid J. H. Johnson............ .... $	375 00
		J. B. McMillan, Treas..............	37 50
	11	F. H. Manning, Supt.	1,500 00
		F. H. Manning, Supt	444 06
		Mr and Mrs Manning	125 00
	12	J. S. Laverty	225 00
		A. W. Williams	150 00
		J. S. Graves, Supt	1,000 00
		J. S. Graves, Supt	707 13
		J. S. Graves	200 00
		Mrs. J. S. Graves	100 00
		Geo Thomason	75 00
		J. H. Johnson, Supt	2,500 00
		Miss S. A Tillinghast	125 00
		Miss A. L. Johnson	200 00
		S. J. Johnson	250 00
		J. F. Bledsoe	150 00
		Osee Roberts	225 00
	15	Miss M. E. Toney	125 00
		W. S. Johnson	175 00
	19	J. S. Laverty	460 52
Nov.	5	A. F. Wood ...	150 00
Dec.	23	Miss S. A. Tillinghast	85 00
1896			
Jan.	7	Express on papers	25
	10	J. B. McMillan, Treas.	37 50
		J. H. Johnson	375 00
		J. H. Johnson, Supt	2,500 00
		J. H. Johnson, Supt	2,027 81
		J. S. Graves, Supt.	957 21
		J. S. Graves, Supt	1,000 00
		J. S. Graves	200 00
		Geo Thomason	75 00
		Mrs. J. S. Graves ..	100 00
		A. F. Wood......	150 00
		J. H. Johnson	700 00
	11	F. H. Manning, Supt.	1,500 00
		F. H. Manning, Supt	1,467 98
		F. H Manning	250 00
		A. W. Williams	150 00
		Miss A. Brockman	125 00
		Miss Lilah McDaniel	125 00
		Miss M. E. Toney	125 00
		W. S. Johnson	175 00
		Osee Roberts	225 00
		J. F. Bledsoe.	150 00
		T. S. McMoney	150 00
		Miss A. L. Johnson	200 00
		S. J. Johnson	250 00
	15	Mrs. F. H. Manning.	125 00
		J. S. Laverty	225 00
Apr.	7	J. B. McMillan, Treas	37 50
	8	F. H. Manning, Supt	1,500 00
		F. H Manning, Supt	1,496 15
		Miss F. L. Leonard.	162 50
		Mrs. F H. Manning.	125 00
		Miss A Brockman	125 00
		Miss L. McDaniel.	125 00
		J. S. Laverty	225 00

1896						$	
April	8	By cash paid J. H. Johnson, Prin			$	2,500	00
		J. H. Johnson, Prin				1,525	50
		J. H. Johnson				375	00
		W. S. Johnson				175	00
		Miss A. L. Johnson				200	00
		S. J. Johnson				250	00
		Miss V. May				162	50
		Miss Grace Ely				195	00
		J. F. Bledsoe				150	00
		T. S. McAloney				150	00
		Miss M. E. Toney				125	00
		Osce Roberts				225	00
		A. F. Wood				150	00
		J. S. Graves, Supt				1,000	00
	11	J. S. Graves, Supt				884	12
		J. T. Graves				290	00
		Mrs. J. S. Graves				100	00
		Geo Thomason				75	00
		F. H. Manning				250	00
		A. W. Williams				150	00
	18	T. S. Plowman and S. J. Bowie				240	00
	24	F. H. Manning, Supt				590	00
May	21	Miss F. Leonard				137	50
June	13	Miss V. May				137	50
	25	Miss Grace Ely				165	00
	29	J. H. Johnson, Supt				2,500	00
July	9	J. H. Johnson, Supt				875	20
		Miss A. L. Johnson				200	00
		S. J. Johnson				250	00
		Miss M. E. Toney				125	00
		Osce Roberts				225	00
		J. H. Johnson				375	00
		T. S McAlonny				150	00
		J. F. Bledsoe				150	00
		Miss L. McDaniel				125	00
		Miss A. Brockman				125	00
		F. H. Manning, Supt				878	39
	10	F. H. Manning, Supt				1,530	00
		A. W. Williams				150	00
		F. H Manning				250	00
		Mrs. F. H. Manning				125	00
		J. S. Laverty				225	00
		J. S. Graves, Supt				1,000	00
		J. S. Graves, Supt				489	19
		Mrs. S. J. Graves				100	00
		J. S. Graves				200	00
		Geo. Thomason				75	00
		W. S. Johnson				175	00
	12	A. F. Wood				150	00
	18	J. B. McMillan				37	50
	21						
		Total			$	97,699	04
		To Balance on hand			$	8,840	22

ALABAMA INSTITUTE FOR THE DEAF.

No.	Name.	County.
1	Alexander, Charles	Dallas
2	Amberson, Earnest.	Elmore
3	Autrey, Emma	Colbert
4	Ballard, Burney.	Lamar
5	Baldwin, Ray	Dekalb
6	Barley, Ada.	Madison
7	Basden, Docia.	Colbert
8	Basden, Gilbert	Colbert
9	Bell, Pauline.	Lowdnes
10	Bennet, Mary	Calhoun
11	Benagh, Hill	Limestone
12	Benagh, Julia	Limestone
13	Black, Linnie	Dekalb
14	Blaylock, Leona.	Wilcox
15	Blansit, Alice	Dekalb
16	Blansit, Della	Dekalb
17	Blansit, John	DeKalb
18	Blevins, James	Cherokee
19	Bledsoe, Arthur	Dale
20	Bozeman, Jessie.	Dallas
21	Brannon, Willie.	Talladega
22	Brizendine, Maud	Jefferson
23	Brocato, Joe.	Jefferson
24	Bridges, Octavia	Cherokee
25	Brust, Lottie.	Madison
26	Carre, May.	Calhoun
27	Caldwell, Chalmar	Clay
28	Caroway, James	Lamar
29	Cagle, Henry.	Lawrence
30	Canoles, Roy	Jefferson
31	Chandler, Oscar	Etowah
32	Crabb, Florence.	Madison
33	Crabb, Joe	Madison
34	Crabb, Robert	Madison
35	Crapps, Andrew.	Monroe
36	Crapps, Sallie.	Monroe
37	Daly, Harry.	Jefferson
38	Delay, Agnes.	Jefferson
39	Davenport, James	Pike
40	Dickinson, Nellie	Pike
41	Dollar, Belle	Randolph
42	Dorlan, Philetus	Mobile
43	Dorlan, Viola	Mobile
44	Dobing, Alice.	Walker
45	Elrod, Henry.	Jefferson
46	Finnegan, Joe.	Talladega
47	Fleming, Jettie	Clarke
48	Folmar, Pearl	Pike
49	Fountain, Joe	Perry
50	Freeman, Minnie.	Madison
51	Gilder, Lula.	Choctaw
52	Hall, Borrell	Shelby
53	Hamilton, Fannie	St. Clair

LIST OF PUPILS, DEAF—Continued.

No.	NAME.	COUNTY
54	Harris, Alice.	Marion
55	Hayne, Effie	Elmore
56	Harper, Herman	Shelby
57	Heaton, Asa	Jefferson
58	Hill, Luther	Franklin
59	Horn, Emory	Clay
60	Horn, Martin	Clay
61	Hickman, Nettie.	Talladega
62	Hughy, Dovie.	Limestone
63	Jarrell, Ada.	Chambers
64	Johnson, Ida.	Coffee
65	Johnson, John.	Coffee
66	Johnson, Mattie.	Chambers
67	Johnson, Willie.	Pike
68	King, Bessie.	Walker
69	King, Sallie	Walker
70	Kimbell, Morris.	Clarke
71	Kirkland, Patty	Morgan
72	Kirkland, Pat.	Morgan
73	Kimbrough, Dan	Franklin
74	Kinghten, Ed.	Choctaw
75	Koenigsthal, Arthur.	Dallas
76	Landers, Lee	Colbert
77	Landrum, Hugh	Dallas
78	Lemons, Jesse	Talladega
79	Levy, Ernest	Jefferson
80	Logan, Dee	Dallas
81	Lovelace, Emma.	Lauderdale
82	Martin, Homer	Bullock
83	Marimon, James.	Marshall
84	Matthews, Lucile.	Talladega
85	McCutchen, Maud.	Madison
86	McLendon, Luther	Jefferson
87	McCord, Chase.	Montgomery
88	McKendree, Lizzie	Tallapoosa
89	McCrosky, Fred.	Morgan
90	Mitchell, Buck.	Tuscaloosa
91	Mitchell, Dave.	Tuscaloosa
92	Middlebrooks, Ben.	Pike
93	Morris, Estin.	Tallapoosa
94	Moore, Pearl.	Chambers
95	Morgan, Victoria.	Bullock
96	Mullen, Mary.	Perry
97	Nelley, Pace.	St. Clair
98	Parks, Sallie.	Pike
99	Patterson, Billy	Clay
100	Peters, Andy.	Jackson
101	Peters, William.	Jackson
102	Phillips, Annie.	Etowah
103	Pollard, Ed.	Marshall
104	Powe, Mary	Talladega
105	Priebe, Bernard	Talladega
106	Pugh, Mitchell	Tallapoosa
107	Pritchett, Mattie	Calhoun
108	Quarles, Dolph	Russell
109	Quarles, Willie	Russell

LIST OF PUPILS, DEAF—Continued

No.	NAME.	COUNTY.
110	Ray, Maggie	Montgomery
111	Ray, Minnie	Clay
112	Ray, Winnie	Clay
113	Rice, Jesse	DeKalb
114	Richards, Ellie	Chambers
115	Robinson, Foster	Limestone
116	Roach, Etoile	Lauderdale
117	Rhoden, Ulysses	Lawrence
118	Ruppert, Winnie	Jefferson
119	Sanders, Gertrude	Elmore
120	Seahorn, Jennie	Talladega
121	Sewell, Henry	Elmore
122	Smith, Stonewall	Talladega
123	Steadham, Ronnie	Calhoun
124	Striplin, Hiram	Randolph
125	Stephens, Edgar	Dallas
126	Sullivan, Jesse	Jefferson
127	Sullivan, John	Jefferson
128	Sullivan, Pink	Jefferson
129	Sowell, Willie	Limestone
130	Tant, Emily	Talladega
131	Tidwell, Sena	Walker
132	Turnham, Maggie	Chambers
133	Teawick, James	Dale
134	Underwood, Lawrence	Lauderdale
135	Vann, Annie	Talladega
136	Vines, Ada	Jefferson
137	Vines, Eugene	Jefferson
138	Vickers, Nathan	Henry
139	Waston, Ampsy	Cherokee
140	Waston, Robert	Talladega
141	Ware, Herman	Tallapoosa
142	Walters, Evern	Montgomery
143	Williams, Atty	Marshall
144	Wolf, Maggie	DeKalb
145	Wolfe, Annie	Calhoun
146	Wolfe, Helen	Calhoun
147	Wolfe, Wash	Calhoun
148	Wright, Estelle	Randolph
149	Yeargan, Warren	Chambers
150	Yielding, Estelle	Jefferson
151	Young, John	DeKalb

ALABAMA ACADEMY FOR THE BLIND.

List of Pupils Enrolled Since Date of Last Report.

No.	Name.	County.
1	Abbott, Mary K	Jefferson
2	Ashburn, Ella	Morgan
3	Averett, Edwin	Russell
4	Baggett, Sallie	Monroe
5	Bates, Winona	Bibb
6	Beeson, Mattie	Jackson
7	Berry, James	Tallapoosa
8	Blair, Hugh	Madison
9	Bloodworth, Leona	Blount
10	Bowles, Annie Bell	Calhoun
11	Camp, Nannie E	Talladega
12	Camp, John H. A	Talladega
13	Carlisle, Lucinda	Jackson
14	Clardy, Lou	Calhoun
15	Clarkson, William	Jefferson
16	Cobb Robert	Clarke
17	Cotnam, Nora	DeKalb
18	Davis, Caledonia	Henry
19	Davis, Emily	Shelby
20	Dill, Chris C	Fayette
21	Dudley, Lonnie	Randolph
22	England, Clifford	Choctaw
23	Ennis, Tullie O	Henry
24	Franks, Jasper U	Limestone •
25	Frye, Maggie	Monroe
26	Grogan, Clarence	Clarke
27	Hacker, Sallie	Limestone
28	Hacker, Larkin,	Limestone
29	Hagood, Rufus	Jefferson
30	Hall, Lily	Jackson
31	Hulsey, John B	Marion
32	Kemp, Thomas	Jefferson
33	Kennedy, Wm. H	Elmore
34	King, David D	Bullock
35	Knight, Clay	Jackson
36	Krentzman, Bessie	Bibb
37	Lee, Daisy	Talladega
38	Lochridge, J. R	Talladega
39	Lovelace, B. P	Lauderdale
40	Lowry, John	Lamar
41	McCullars, John T	Walker
42	McCullom, Eugenia	Clay
43	McEachem,	Tallapoosa
44	McGehee, Jessie	Calhoun
45	Malone, Ella	Mobile
46	Malone, Thomas	Mobile
47	Meadows, Huldah	Elmore
48	Merritt, Edward A.	Geneva
49	Middleton, Rosalie	Lee
50	Mobley, Lizzie	Calhoun
51	Monday, Eugene	Marshall
52	Moog, Felix V	Mobile
53	Moore, Earnest	Coffee

LIST OF PUPILS, BLIND—Continued.

No.	NAME.	COUNTY.
54	Moore, T. A.	Tallapoosa
55	Morgan, Margaret	Calhoun
56	Orrell, Edwin	Mobile
57	Owen, Arthur	Randolph
58	Parks, R. L.	Jackson
59	Paschal, Florence	Montgomery
60	Patterson, Jasper	Colbert
61	Piercy, Lily	Henry
62	Pinson, Hixie	Jefferson
63	Pinson, Eula	Jefferson
64	Pinson, Maud	Jefferson
65	Pinson, Gregory	Jefferson
66	Pinson, Mildred	Jefferson
67	Pinson, Rose	Marshall
68	Pinson, James	Marshall
69	Pinson, Minnie	Tallapoosa
70	Pinson, Osce	Tallapoosa
71	Pinson, Alfous	Tallapoosa
72	Pittman, Malcolm	Dale
73	Powers, Venie	Fayette
74	Prince, Maggie	Limestone
75	Prince, Ida	Limestone
76	Prince, Leonard	Winston
77	Purswell, Maxie	Henry
78	Reeves, Parlee	Clarke
79	Reeves, Virg'l	Lawrence
80	Rigsby, Hamp	Chambers
81	Roberts, Cora	Madison
82	Roebuck, Alfred	Shelby
83	Rush, Mary Alberta	Lee
84	Rush, Clarence	Lee
85	Russell, Claude	DeKalb
86	Ryan, Jennie	Jackson
87	Scott, Jefferson	Calhoun
88	Shealey, Henry	Talladega
89	Sheppard, Mary	Tallapoosa
90	Stirly, Henry	Clay
91	Sims, Minnie	Jefferson
92	Smith, Ada	Chambers
93	Smith, Ruth	Chambers
94	Snow, Thomas	Madison
95	Stewart, Jenny	Crenshaw
96	Sudduth, Mercer	Fayette
97	Swindell, John	Lauderdale
98	Thomas, John	Lauderdale
99	Tomlinson, Barney	Chambers
100	Williamson, Theodore	St. Clair
101	Yarbrough, Blanche	Lee
102	York, Haywood	Jackson
103	Young, John	Lauderdale
104	Young, Iris	Morgan

ALABAMA NEGRO SCHOOL FOR DEAF-MUTES AND BLIND.

No.	NAME.	COUNTY.
	DEAF-MUTES.	
1	Banks, William....	Bibb
2	Braselton, Joseph	Bibb
3	Darthard, Lacey	Lawrence
4	Fain, Mary....	Talladega
5	Fitten, Elizabeth..............	Macon
6	Fitten, Lou	Macon
7	Fitten, Zetta	Macon
8	Fitten, Britton..........	Macon
9	Flannegan, James.	Jefferson
10	Glenn, Carrie	Montgomery
11	Graham, Cap	Talladega
12	Hill, Tillman......	Talladega
13	Hall, George................	Macon
14	Harvey, Jack	Montgomery
15	Harris, Maria............	Limestone
16	Hops, Bud	Talladega
17	Jackson, Walter.	Calhoun
18	Jackson, Francis ...	Jefferson
19	Johnson, Leona...	Talladega
20	Kimble, Mason........	Morgan
21	Mathews, Lulu	Jefferson
22	Mathews, Willie	Jefferson
23	Meadows, Douglas....	Chambers
24	McCullough, Mary	Talladega
25	Morris, Willie	Talladega
26	Nunn, Josephine	Jefferson
27	Neville, Laura	Morgan
28	Patton, Benjamin	Lauderdale
29	Ried, Carabell	Chambers
30	Sharper, Sterling	Macon
31	Wade, William	Lauderdale
32	Walker, Henry	Greene
33	Williams, Charley .	Jefferson
	BLIND.	
1	Allen, Thomas	Jefferson
2	Abernathy, Fredrick.	Colbert
3	Banks, Burton	Bibb
4	Banks, Henry	Bibb
5	Canner, Henry	Pickens
6	Casper, Martin	Talladega
7	Dunn, Carrie	Clay
8	Edwards, James	Jefferson
9	Floyd, Maggie....	Morgan
10	Foggy, Luckie.	Talladega
11	Gardner, Henry	Dallas
12	Gardner, James.................	Jefferson
13	Gaiter, Anna	Talladega
14	Garrett, Evans	Talladega

50

No.	Name.	County
15	Henderson, Lola,	Bullock
16	Harris, Willie	Sumter
17	Horton, Cornelia	Jefferson
18	Hillard, Austin	Jefferson
19	Jenkins, Katie	Talladega
20	Kellogg, Milton	Bibb
21	Lacey, Lewis	Jefferson
22	Lewis, John	Montgomery
23	Long, Joseph	Tuscaloosa
24	Madden, Ambrose	Colbert
25	Mitchell, Nettie	Montgomery
26	McKenzie, Arnell	Jefferson
27	McCondichie, James	Wilcox
28	McDow, Mary	Etowah
29	Pope, Mattie	Talladega
30	Price, Elisha	Montgomery
31	Ried, Heath	Escambia
32	Riddle, Thomas	Greene
33	Shed, Ross	St. Clair
34	Taylor, John	Montgomery
35	Townsend, Israel	Limestone
36	Underwood, Isabella	Perry
37	Walker, Sallie	Talladega
38	Wilson, Rena	Talladega
39	Young, Andrew	Lowndes

CIRCULAR OF INFORMATION.

There are on the rolls of these schools about one hundred twenty-six (126) Deaf pupils; sixty-five (65) Blind pupils; and in the Negro School for Deaf and Blind, fifty (50) pupils.

There are in the State at least three hundred (300) Deaf and Blind children, of suitable age, who ought to be in school.

Less than half of those who are entitled to the benefits of these schools have availed themselves of the opportunity afforded them to obtain an education and equip themselves for the battle of life, and this in spite of the fact that *board and tuition are free.*

Generally parents are anxious for their seeing and hearing children to go to school, and frequently practice great self-denial in order to send them. Is it not strange then, that these unfortunate deaf and blind children, whose only hope of success in life depends upon their being educated, should be kept at home to grow up in ignorance, and that too, when they can be educated at less cost to their parents than their more fortunate brothers and sisters.

Parents assign many reasons for this unnatural conduct. They are unwilling to be parted from the child for nine months in the year, admitting at the same time that they can do nothing for the child at home. They choose to condemn the child to a life of ignorance and deprivation rather than part with it for a few years, giving as a reason for such conduct that their love for the child is so great that they cannot bear the separation. We cannot refrain from questioning the wisdom of such love.

They do not like to send their children to a charitable institution; while in one sense these schools are charitable institutions, in that they are provided and supported by a generous people; in another and broader sense they are not "charities."

In their support and maintenance the State is simply performing a duty to itself.

In conception and in fact, these are purely *educational* institutions, and in no sense "Homes" or "Asylums" for the destitute.

LOCATION.

These schools are located in the town of Talladega, in Talladega County, in North-East Alabama. No better place in the State could be chosen for the location of schools of this character. Talladega being noted as one of the healthiest towns in the State—high above the sea, surrounded by mountains, the air is pure and bracing; easy of access, having three railroads bringing us within four hours run of Montgomery, and in three hours to Birmingham.

The "Institute for the Deaf" is within a quarter of a mile of the public square of the town, south-east from the square.

The "Academy for the Blind" is just one-half mile east of the "Institute for the Deaf," on the same street.

The "School for Negro Deaf-Mutes and Blind," is located one-half mile south of the "Academy for the Blind" and is at the intersection of Fourth Street with the Chandler's Springs Road.

INSTITUTE FOR THE DEAF

The property of the State known as the "Institute for the Deaf," is on East Street, within a quarter of a mile of the public square of the city of Talladega, embraces seventeen acres of land, five substantial brick buildings, two, three and four stories high.

The Main Building is a four-story brick structure, with slate roof; in the building are the girls' dormitories, sitting-rooms, sewing-rooms, bath-rooms. Also teachers' and officers' quarters, reception rooms, parlors, and the Superintendent's office and apartments.

Immediately in the rear of the Main Building, and connected with it, is a two-story brick building with slate roof; containing kitchen, store-room, bath-rooms, lavatories, etc.

To the right of the Main Building, is the School Building, a three-story brick building with slate roof. Here are the class rooms and chapel.

To the left of the Main Building is a four-story brick building with slate roof, containing boys' dormitories, study-halls, sitting-rooms and bath-rooms.

In the rear of the Main Building, and at a little distance from it, is the "Mechanical Department," a two-story brick building with metal roof; in this building we have a steam boiler and engine to furnish power for wood-working machinery, printing-presses, sewing-machines, etc. The printing-office, cabinet-shop and shoe-shop are all in this building. A steam laundry, perfect in its appointments, occupies one end of the ground floor. There are, in addition to these, several frame buildings on the place affording room for stables, water-closets, etc.

The Institute is supplied with gas from the city gas works, and with water from the city water works.

The fire protection is ample, there being two double hydrants in the yard. The school owns its own hose-reel and five hundred feet of best three-inch "White Anchor" hose. And in term time a fire company, composed of deaf boys well drilled, gives to all on the place a very satisfactory sense of security from danger by fire.

Of the seventeen acres of land, the front yard containing ten or twelve acres, is set in grass, and is full of fine forest trees— oak, elm, maple, etc. In the rear, and on either side, are play grounds for the children, also flower and vegetable gardens.

The sanitary conditions are carefully looked after; the mortuary record showing but four deaths since the establishment of the schools, in 1858, the facts being that in each of these cases there was chronic or hereditary trouble before entering the school.

ACADEMY FOR THE BLIND.

This property lies one-half mile east of the Institute for the Deaf, on the same street. It consists of six acres of land and three handsome, new brick buildings.

The Main Building, an imposing three-story brick building with slate and metal roof, stands on the highest ground and near the centre of the lot. In this building we have the chapel, dining room, boys' and girls' dormitories, sitting-rooms, study-halls and music-rooms, boys' and girls' hospitals, teachers and officers' quarters, reception rooms and Superintendent's business office.

To the right, and in front of the Main Building, is the School Building, two stories high, with basement, containing class-rooms, music-rooms, library, etc., also boys' dormitory, and sitting-room.

Immediately to the right of the Main Building, is a two-story brick building with slate roof, containing shops, laundry-room, bath-room, and boiler-room.

All three of these buildings are comfortably heated by steam, and lighted with gas. We are also supplied with water from the city water works, and have an abundant supply for all purposes.

The site is a commanding one, although now the grounds are tastefully laid off and are in good condition. Here, as at the Institute for the Deaf, the sanitary conditions are carefully loooked after, the best evidence of which is that we have had but little sickness and no deaths.

SCHOOL FOR NEGRO DEAF AND BLIND.

At this school is a handsome three-story brick building, covered with slate and trimmed with stone, comfortably furnished throughout. The lot embraces fifteen (15) acres, and is a fine site for a public building. It will accommodate seventy-five pupils.

OBJECT OF THE SCHOOL.

As before stated, these are schools, pure and simple. They were established and are supported by the State, in recognition of the fact that deaf and blind children are as much entitled to an education as their hearing and seeing brothers and sisters, and while they are in one sense charitable institutions, they are not to be considered charities in the ordinary acceptation of the term, and in no sense *asylums*.

Those who have lost simply hearing or sight and retain their mental faculties unimpared, do not ask the State to provide for them beyond the necessary equipment for the struggle of life, and it is for this purpose that these Institutions are main-tained. Idiotic or helpless deaf or blind children have no place in these schools.

When children are received in these schools and it is ascer-tained that they are incapable of receiving instruction, they at once sent home, in simple justice to the people who give their support to the institutions as schools.

It is the object of these schools to give intelligence, pleasure, and happiness to a class which, without aid, must necessarily live in darkness; to make useful, self-supporting, contributing citizens of a class which, without help, would in most cases, be dependent upon charity.

It is proposed to give the pupils in these schools a practical English education, the course of study being very much the same as that in the common public schools of the State, including Language, Composition, Grammar, Rhetoric, Geography (physical and political,) Mathematics, Physiology, Anatomy, Natural Philosophy and Mental and Moral Science.

With the deaf especial attention is paid to the English Language, as it presents with them, the first as well as the greatest difficulty, for the reason that it is to them as much a foreign language as French or German to an English speaking, hearing child.

With the blind much attention is given to Music, there being no means by which a talented blind person can more readily or more pleasantly make a living than by following the profession of music. The idea, however, that all blind persons are musical, is as fallacious as it is wide-spread; the proportion of natural musicians among the blind is no greater than among the seeing, and to think that it is, is only another evidence that many people believe the blind to be precocious and peculiar when they are neither.

In all of these schools there is a Mechanical or Industrial Department, where the pupils are given trades, by means of which they may become entirely, or in part, self-supporting.

At the Institute for the Deaf the boys are taught general habits of industry; they receive special instruction at the following trades: Printing, Shoe-Making, Cabinet and Carpenter Work, Painting, Vegetable and Landscape Gardening; the girls are taught House-Work, Plain and Machine Sewing, Dress-Making, Cutting and Fitting, Crocheting, House-Cleaning, etc.

At the Academy for the Blind the boys are taught Mattress-Making, Cane-Seating, Collar-Making, Basket-Making, Piano-Tuning and Repairing, etc. The girls also learn Cane-Seating, in addition to Sewing, Knitting, Crocheting, House-Cleaning, etc.

These several arts and trades are run solely for the purpose of benefitting the pupils, and while there is some little revenue from some of the branches of trade, they are without exception run at an expense; but this is not allowed to stand in the way of the best interests of the pupils. The provision made for instruction in each branch is first-class, the trades being carried on in the same way, and viewed in the same light as the literary and musical departments. We consider the industrial department equally as important as the educational department. The average deaf-mute or blind person, who has no trade to rely upon, is almost certain to make a failure in life. Many such, who could never hope to command more than from eight to fifteen dollars per month, as common laborers, with their trades learned in school often make that much per week.

"THE WILSON SHOP."

The "Wilson Shops," at the Institute for the Deaf, are now in complete running order with all the latest improved wood-working machinery and a new automatic engine.

RULES, TERMS OF ADMISSION, ETC.

The following Rules, Terms of Admission, etc., apply to The Institute for the Deaf, The Academy for the Blind and The School for Negro Deaf-Mutes and Blind:

1. The benefits of these schools are free to all deaf and blind children in Alabama, whose hearing or sight is so impaired as to prevent their being taught in the ordinary public schools. Board, Books, Tuition and Medical Attendance are furnished free. Parents or friends must furnish Clothing and pay Traveling Expenses. Clothing must be plain, substantial and warm and every article plainly marked.

2. The minimum age for admission is eight years, and none will be received under that age without special action on the part of the Board of Trustees.

3. The applicant must be of sound mind, and free from such chronic disease as would prevent study.

4. The time allowed by law for a pupil to remain in school is eight years; the Board however may extend the time, if in their judgment the progress of the pupil justifies it. The Board reserves the right to discharge any pupil at any time for cause; and in no case will a child be continued in school after it is fully ascertained that he can make no futher progress in his studies.

5. The school session lasts forty weeks, beginning about the fifteenth of September. A pupil entering the school at any time during the year, is expected to remain until the session closes, and will not be allowed to withdraw, unless for some very good reason. Nothing so interrupts the work and tends to demoralize the classes as taking the pupil from school before the close of the session. Any pupil taken home during the session, without the consent of the Board, forfeits the privilege of attending the schools.

6. It is very important that all pupils enter school at the beginning of the session. If a pupil comes in late, he is behind in his class, and not only does little good himself, but prevents the class from making the progress it should make, by dividing the time of teacher. See that your child comes promptly at the beginning of the school and gets a fair start with his class.

7. Boys are put at a trade as soon as they are large enough to work and have discretion enough to handle tools without danger to themselves. In selecting a trade, we always, as far as possible, consult the individual taste and talent of the boys and the wishes of his parents. All pupils who are large enough are required to work at some sort of manual labor, and there is no deviation from this rule, except in cases of physical disability, which are very rare.

8. The parents and friends of the pupils are at liberty to visit the children at any time, but when making these visits they cannot be entertained at the school.

9. All letters and packages should be directed in care of the "Institution for the Deaf," or the "Academy for the Blind," or "School for Negro Deaf-Mutes and Blind."

10. Any further information desired can be had by addressing.

J. H. Johnson, Principal.

Talladega, Ala

www.ingramcontent.com/pod-product-compliance
Lightning Source LLC
Chambersburg PA
CBHW031453270326
41930CB00007B/980
9783741177767